A DAY AT THE BOWLING ALLEY WITH FRIENDS

...YELL NO! LET'S GO!

CHRISTOPHER DAVID

To order additional copies of this book, contact:
Xlibris
1-888-795-4274
www.Xlibris.com
Orders@Xlibris.com

A DAY AT THE BOWLING ALLEY WITH FRIENDS

Michael, Amelia, Sydney, Ally, Jessica, and Nikki

Went for a walk one day

They looked for a bowling alley to play

When they finally found one, oh boy, did they have fun!

New friends Jessica and Niki came along this time

While homework was being done by Josh and Sky

HAWKEYE

They bowled some games and had a bunch of fun

While they played and enjoyed some bubble gum

As they were bowling some
games alone a bully came

He had some prescription drugs
and said, "Try It! It's OK !"

SNACKS

Pizza   Nachos
Popcorn   Pretzels
Cotton Candy   Caramel Apples
Candy   Soda Pop
Chips   Lemonade

**Michael said in a loud voice,
"YELL NO! LET'S GO!"**

As Amelia went to get help

Because of Michael's loud voice and Amelia going to get help

The bully turned coward and he left the bowling alley

When Amelia came back

The friends gathered at the bowling ball rack

Michael said, "Remember what Uncle taught us!"

When there are bullies, danger, drugs or violence always

...YELL NO! LET'S GO!

Printed in the United States
By Bookmasters